# a gi

*This book
is dedicated to all of us,
who by helping each other
can make our planet
paradise
here and now.*

# How To HELP Your-*Self*

## *by Raja*

Published by
HELP Books International
P.O. Box 929
Wimbledon - London
SW19 2AX - UK
e-mail: mail@helpbooksint.com
www.helpbooksint.com

**ISBN 0 9535 7777 5**

How To HELP Your-*Self* is based on The HELP Book

*Printed in Scotland by Omnia Books Ltd.*

# —— CONTENTS ——

# INTRODUCTION

*The most important lesson you can
learn in life is how to help your Self.*

Before you read this book, draw an imaginary circle around your current capacity to help yourself. Now, as you read The Seven Lessons of **How To HELP Your-*Self*,** your capacity will expand - increase daily.

The more you learn how to help your Self, the more you will accomplish in every area of your life. There are no limits to what you can create and become. You are only limited by your capacity to help yourself.

The purpose of this book is to guide you in

fulfilling all your needs, dreams and desires. But how can you actually meet all your needs, manifest your dreams and fulfil your desires? By learning how to help your Self.

The most important lesson you can learn in life is how to help your Self. Why? By helping yourself you stay alive, grow, prosper and procreate. Helping yourself is the most primal and powerful action in life. The way to fulfil all your needs, dreams and desires is by mastering how to help your Self.

Although this book is called *How To HELP Your-Self* it could also be titled *The Way To Paradise*. By reading this book you are learning how to meet all your needs and create a living condition of Paradise - here and now.

Is the way to Paradise too simple to be true?

The content of this book is simple - yet it has the potential to take you from here to Paradise. Is it really possible for you to live in a condition of Paradise? Yes.

How To HELP Your-*Self* is based on Seven Lessons. In each lesson you will learn how to meet all your physical and spiritual needs - as they arise.

When *all* your needs are fulfilled, you will experience peace and ease - the precondition to Paradise. Living in a constant condition of peace and ease *is* Paradise.

You may think that you already know how to help your Self. But if you are not living in a constant condition of Paradise, you have yet to learn how to help your Self.

Learning how to help your Self never stops. Helping yourself is the way to meet all your challenges on ever expanding levels. In fact, the more you apply The Seven Lessons in this book, the more, caring, creative and comfortable you will become in every area of your life.

To help yourself is to love yourself.

Every time you help yourself, you release the most powerful force in creation - *love*. Knowing how to help yourself is the way to love yourself. The more you help yourself, the more love you feel.

In this way you will feel fully filled and love will overflow in your life. When this happens you will turn your focus from yourself to fellow human beings. How To HELP Your-*Self* will then take on new meanings and purpose.

You see, in life you will encounter several cycles of growth and at each stage and age there are new challenges. The more you are called upon to do in this life, the more you will need to learn how to help your Self.

In *The HELP Book\**, I explained in depth - The HELP Process and its incredible potential to help individuals, groups and organizations at every level.

How To HELP Your-*Self* is an excellent introduction to The HELP Process and is the result of over a thousand HELP Seminars. This book is being used as a work book by students, teachers, trainers, therapists, self-help groups and so on.

~ 4 ~

# INTRODUCTION

How To HELP Your-*Self* will guide you through every step of The HELP Process. This is learned, taught and practiced via The Seven Lessons of HELP - In Practice.

The HELP Process is a new discovery - Sacred Science. It presents universal truths which illuminate the whole of human nature. As such, it may challenge your current way of living. I suggest you read this book slowly, studying and practicing each of The Seven Lessons systematically.

The following Seven Lessons have helped countless people from all walks of life to fulfil their needs, dreams and desires.

How To HELP Your-*Self* will help you to live the life you really desire - becoming your constant companion for life.

# THE FOUNDATIONS

## OF

## HELP

*The way to create real and lasting*
*peace and ease is by nurturing*
*the foundations of your life.*
The HELP Book

*The Foundations of HELP
nurture both the physical and spiritual
needs of a human being* .......

The First Lesson is to learn the true priorities in your life. This may sound obvious, but you will be surprised as to how many of you are running from pillar-to-post every day.

You may already have priorities in place or you may be searching for them. Some of you may even have fulfilled your priorities, and yet you do not live in a condition of peace and ease.

Your priorities, are your focus in life. What you focus on with your mind, money, energy and faith determines the condition of your life.

What are the priorities in your life?

What are you focusing on; money, property, power, fame, fashion, beauty, spirituality and success? Is that what you really need?

By focusing on such priorities, you may become very *successful,* but you will be living out your days as a slave. Your priorities will lead you to Slavery or Freedom. A free man or woman is a slave to nothing and no one.

If you are not a free man or woman, then you have yet to learn about priorities. Whether you are free or a slave will be seen in the way you live. A slave suffers from anxiety and burden, whereas a free human being lives in peace and ease.

The aim is to move from Slavery to Freedom by choosing *true* priorities. I am going to ask you a question. What are the true priorities in life?

By knowing the true priorities in your life, you will focus on fulfilling the *real* needs of being human. When all your real needs are met, you will feel at peace and ease. If you are not living in a condition of peace and ease, then you will need to question your focus in life.

Many of you focus your entire lives on false priorities and never question why? Look closely at the lives of your parents, teachers, preachers and politicians. What do you see?

The majority of you are living in trouble and strife as a result of focusing on false priorities. Even the wisest and the wealthiest among you often do not live in peace and ease. Why?

At this point I am going to make a basic separation between priorities and foundations. A priority can be to make more money, whereas a foundation supports your very existence.

Many of you are focusing on priorities, but are unaware of the foundations of your life. The way forward is for each one of you to focus on the very foundations of being human.

So what are the foundations of your life?

Again, this question sounds simple, but what are they? The obvious thing to say is that you already know. If you know what they are, then write them down now.

Be sure that you are willing to devote your life towards your chosen foundations. After all, you do not want to build your future on weak foundations. What you want is to build your life on foundations that are above and beyond doubt.

All human beings have the same foundations and yet we don't know what they are. Despite all our knowledge and wisdom, humanity has yet to discover the very foundations of a human being.

Let me tell you. The foundations of a human being are *Health, Home, Family and Work.* "So what?", you say, "We all have health, a home, family and work." Yes, you may know these words and use them often - yet not know that *together* they are the very foundations of a human being. You see, that is the fundamental new discovery.

The point is that these are not random priorities, but the very foundations of Human Evolution and Life Procreation - H.E.L.P.* That is why they are called The Foundations of HELP.

To appreciate the significance of this discovery, you have to *re-learn* the role of Health, Home, Family and Work in your life. Focusing your life on these foundations is altogether a completely new understanding of priorities.

The Foundations of HELP are the roots of life. All life forms depend on these foundations to evolve and procreate. These foundations connect human nature with Nature - Mother Earth. They are the core foundations of our existence.

To find out if these are the true foundations of your life, choose a need. You will find that it originates from one or more of these foundations. All your needs originate from these foundations.

By focusing your priorities on your Health, Home, Family and Work, you will meet every need

* H.E.L.P. - Taken from The HELP Book

of being human. *When human beings focus on these foundations, they will meet every need of being human.*

The Foundations of HELP enable you to find and fulfil every need of being human. Just as a tree needs strong roots to grow and bear fruit, a human being needs healthy foundations to live and prosper.

If your life is based on false priorities, then many of your real needs have not been met. When your real needs are not being met, there will be anxiety and burden in your life.

Anxiety and burden cause pain and in due course *dis-ease*. The pain of dis-ease will need pain killers. To ease the pain you will *chase* pleasure, power, success, spirituality, money, fame and so on. These will become the priorities in your life. When that happens, your real needs will be neglected.

Prolonged neglect of your real needs will result in the use of addictions and attachments to cope with the pain. All addictions and attachments come from denial of your real needs. Are you addicted or attached in any way? If so, you are a slave to false priorities that force you to neglect your real needs. As slaves serve their masters, you will serve your false priorities with addictions and attachments.

False priorities have made you a slave to your addictions and attachments. You are not a slave to other people, but to the false priorities in your mind. Your priorities are in control of your life. Many of you think that you are free because you live in a free country. No you are not. To be free you must free yourself from false priorities. How do you do that?

All addictions and attachments are overcome by focusing on The Foundations of HELP. By finding and fulfilling your real needs coming from these foundations, you will experience real freedom and wellbeing.

Wellbeing is when all your real needs are met. Your Health, Home, Family and Work are the wells of your *wellbeing*. As you focus on The Foundations of HELP, all your needs will be met. Are you running from pillar-to-post trying to maintain your home, family, health and work, yet your fundamental needs are not being met?

If this is so, you are not listening to your real needs coming from these foundations. Instead, you are abusing your Health, Home, Family and Work in order to serve your false priorities.

The pursuit of false priorities will cause anxiety and burden - Slavery. By changing your priorities, you change your mind from Slavery to Freedom. You will be in control of your life.

The more you focus your mind, money, energy and faith on your Health, Home, Family and Work, the easier your life will become. When all your physical and spiritual needs are met, you will feel peace and ease - the precondition to Paradise. At this stage you will understand how each foundation interacts with another constantly.

The Foundations of HELP are like the roots of a tree. They are intertwined, so that the condition of one affects the condition of the others. You need to nurture all foundations *equally* if you are to live in a condition of peace and ease - Paradise.

When I tell people that my life is Paradise, they cannot believe me. Why? Because our species has lived in slavery for so long, that someone living in Paradise is unbelievable. The way to Paradise is simple and practical. Paradise for me is the constant fulfilment of all my physical and spiritual needs.

A human being is both physical and spiritual in nature and the Foundations of HELP nurture both the physical and spiritual needs of a human being. Your Health, Home, Family and Work nurture all your physical and spiritual needs, bringing ease to your body and peace to your mind.

Simply, by nurturing your foundations daily, you will increase peace and ease in your life. I live in constant peace and ease, simply by devoting myself to serving my Health, Home, Family and Work.

So many of you are looking for ways to meet

your physical and spiritual needs but you are overlooking the very foundations of being human. Whatever your race or religion you can devote yourself towards building the foundations of your life - The Foundations of HELP.

These are your foundations of life, the pillars of faith and the fountains of your fortune. My life is a living Paradise, because I am blessed with life, faith and fortune. If you lack anything in life, your foundations are weak. People with weak foundations live poor lives, without faith and fortune.

Invest everything you have in serving your Health, Home, Family and Work. When that happens, God* will bless you over, above and beyond your imagination.

Every day millions of people pray, meditate, and chant to ask God to bless them, yet they continue to suffer and struggle daily. God wants to bless each one of you, but you must live according to the will of God. What is the will of God? *The will*

* God - The omnipresent Infinite Being.
The word 'God' is used in this text as a universal term, not as a religious distinction.

*of God is that you live in peace and ease - Paradise.*

Blessings are God's way of giving you what you need to live in Paradise. By serving your foundations, you serve God who blesses your Health, Home, Family and Work. What is more practical and spiritual than that?

The Foundations of HELP are also The Foundations for building *Pan\* Paradise.* But how do you help billions of people to nurture their Health, Home, Family and Work?

Where do you start? With your Self.

In lessons Four, Five, Six and Seven you will learn in depth how to nurture your Health, Home, Family and Work. The easiest and the fastest way to create Pan Paradise on Earth is for you to focus on your foundations of life.

By helping yourself, you also help every other human being. You will find that every choice you make and every action you perform either helps or harms your Health, Home, Family and Work. In turn,

~ 19 ~

*Pan meaning 'one complete whole.' Taken from the Pan Life Teachings by Raja.

these foundations are intertwined with *everyone* you meet and form the tapestry of your society, country and humanity.

As your understanding of The Foundations of HELP increases, you will become aware that these four foundations are the very bedrock of human cohabitation. The entire human world culture and the future of our species depend on these foundations.

By nurturing your foundations you are helping the whole of humanity. The way to promote world peace and ease is by learning how to help yourself develop your own foundations of life. *The world starts with your Self.*

# ~ Lesson One In Practice ~

**Aim:** To move from Slavery to Freedom - being free from all anxiety and burden. To live in constant peace and ease - Paradise.

**Method:** Change your priorities by focusing *all* your mind, money, energy and faith on your Health, Home, Family and Work. Ask God to guide you, to listen and learn from the real needs coming from these four foundations.

**Practice:** First, release your resistance to finding and fulfilling your real needs to live in constant peace and ease - Paradise. Then choose *one real need daily* from each of The Foundations of HELP and fulfil that need to the fullest. Expect all your needs to be met completely.

**Result:** By nurturing these foundations, you will fulfil your real needs and heal yourself from the dis-ease of addiction and attachment. In this way you will live in constant peace and ease - Paradise.

## ~ Lesson Two ~

# THE PAN PATHWAYS

*All living beings*
*use these pathways all the time*
*to exist and give birth to new beings.*
The HELP Book

*The Pan Pathways*
*are the pathways that channel*
*the power of God into a human being.......*

The Second Lesson is to learn how to exercise your supernatural power. You are born with the supernatural potential to help yourself create whatever you need, dream and desire.

Humans are the most adaptable, rational, creative and intuitive creatures on this planet. So why is it so many of you are barely managing your lives? Even those who are well educated, successful and spiritual do not demonstrate the supernatural powers of being human. Why?

You are created by The Infinite Being - God

and that makes you an act of God. If that is true, you have the potential to exercise the power of God.

How can you exercise the power of God?

You may say, by prayer, meditation, and chanting but that is not the answer. After all, many people in our past and present have used these means and not acted with the power of God.

An act of God is a supernatural event. The one who can truly exercise supernatural power will demonstrate that power in *every* action.

Everything you do is an action. When each action is powered by God, you will help yourself with the supernatural power of being human. This lesson will show you how to exercise your supernatural power in every action.

The power I speak of is not born of money, might, position, possessions, success or fame. These are sources of 'man-made' power used to perform natural actions.

You are learning to perform supernatural

actions, which are powered by the force of God. Many of you are exercising man made power - that is why you are power-less. Others claim to know God, but cannot act with the power of God. Why?

What has happened to your supernatural potential? Your spirit, mind and heart are lying dormant, waiting to come alive. *The Pan Pathways** will free your spirit, mind and heart. Only then will you be able to exercise your God given power.

What are The Pan Pathways?

They are the four universal pathways of *Being, Knowing, Relating* and *Creating.* These four pathways power and govern every action.

All power is exercised in action - now. The Pan Pathways are used in every action, that is why they are called The *Pan* Pathways. By learning how to use these pathways, you will exercise your supernatural potential in every action.

You are a physical and spiritual human being. Just as you work the four limbs of your body to

* The Pan Pathways - Discovered by Raja.

exercise your physical power, the four pathways of Being, Knowing, Relating and Creating work together to exercise your spiritual power.

The Pan Pathway of Being frees your spirit, Knowing awakens your mind, Relating opens your heart and Creating guides you to exercise your supernatural power and purpose in every action.

Imagine what one human being can create and contribute to humanity and the Earth with the power of God. The Pan Pathways are the pathways that channel the power of God -The Infinite Being into a human being.

The Pan Pathways are very powerful.

Before we go further, let me forewarn you that the following explanation will penetrate to the heart of your Being. As such, on the first reading you may feel overwhelmed.

We begin with The Pan Pathway of Being, which connects your Being with God and guides you in being yourself. You do this by separating five illusions from reality in your mind. When your mind is free from illusions, the supernatural power of God will flow into your Being.

*Gain and Loss* is the first illusion. This illusion is born out of the *fear* of not having enough. If your actions are motivated by gain and loss, then you cannot give and receive freely. Anyone dealing in gain and loss will never have enough. To overcome the illusion of gain and loss you must see each and every interaction as a *neutral* event.

Look how you are breathing in and out, without a thought of gain and loss. That is the reality of neutrality. To be free of this illusion replace gain and loss, with the reality of *Neutrality.*

*Success and Failure* is the second illusion. This illusion is born of greed. The 'quest for success' is the endless desire to have more money, materials, power, fame and so on.

Success is like a mirage, and so the desire for more is never satisfied. When that happens, you feel like a failure. Even when you have more than you ever need, you will yearn for more. Are you searching for success and finding failure? If so, replace the illusion of success and failure with the reality of *Contentment.*

*Great and Small* is the third illusion. This illusion comes from lack of Self-worth. The desire to be great is an attempt to reinstate your Self-worth, for instance wanting to be better, richer, faster, bigger, or smarter than anyone else.

The folly of 'greatness' is that there is always someone 'greater' and so you feel 'smaller.' If you are motivated by the illusion of great and small, what you are really looking for is love, respect and recognition. All these will come by reinstating your own Self-worth with the reality that I am that I am.

The next time you feel greater or smaller than anyone, believe that you are no less or more than anyone else. Acknowledge your Self-worth with the reality that *I am that I am.*

*Right and Wrong* is the fourth illusion. This illusion stems from ignorance. An ignorant person casts absolute judgment on what is right and wrong for everyone. Ask yourself is it right or wrong to walk naked down the street? For you it may be wrong, but for someone else it may be right.

The illusion of right and wrong will keep your mind closed and cause you to remain ignorant. To come out of ignorance, use your discretion to decide what is appropriate for *you*. When you feel a prisoner of your judgement, replace it with the reality of your own *Discretion*.

*Heaven and Hell* is the fifth and final illusion. This illusion is rooted in disbelief - the disbelief that God is with you. The purpose of all religions is to reunite man with God. The reality is that God is with you here and now......*but are you with God?*

In the chase to get from here to Heaven, you are forsaking the moment of being with God - now. There is nothing in 'Heaven or Hell' that is not here on Earth. Heaven and Hell are not destinations but the conditions you create. Heaven is not 'a place', it is the reality of 'being with God now'.

The next time you are threatened by the illusion of Heaven and Hell, remember that you are here with God *Now*. This is the *ultimate reality*.

Now look closely at your motivation for choosing your clothes, career, car, home, friends, partner and so on. Ask yourself: Are your needs, dreams and desires originating from the realm of illusion or reality?

Is your life based on illusion or reality?

If your motivation originates from the realm of illusion, then you are living a lie and will be forced to tell lies, cheat and steal.

By replacing the five illusions with reality, falsehood will vanish and truth will enter your Being. With your mind cleansed of falsehood, you will be empowered to live a life of truth. Use the realms of illusion as your reality check.

The Pan Pathway of Knowing is the way to eternal freedom. It will set you free to envision, imagine, reason and think your own thoughts. You do this by practicing the four ways of Knowing - *Being Told, Reasoning, Imagining and Direct Knowing.*

*Being Told* is the first way of Knowing. Almost everything you know comes from your parents, teachers, peers and society. You learnt by being told how to cook, clean, eat, read, write, speak and by being shown via the five senses. Being shown is the most practiced way of Knowing, because you can see and touch the physical world. But how much of what you were told is actually true?

Many of you are caught in a cycle of suffering because you do not question what you are taught or told to do. Break this pattern by questioning the information that is coming into your mind.

*Reasoning* is the second way of Knowing. By reasoning you make links between questions and answers, choices and actions, cause and effect.

Almost every choice you make involves reasoning. What is the reason behind your choice to read this book? Reasoning has helped you to survive and stay alive and now it is helping you to become Self-motivated.

Pure reason is very enlightening, but it has limitations as it is confined to your existing knowledge. Reasoning alone cannot inspire you to create or discover that which you do not know.

*Imagining* is the third way of Knowing. It is seeing with your 'mind's eye'. Imagining helps you to see beyond 'what is' to 'what can be'.

Are you one of the millions who feel trapped in your circumstances. If so, use your imagination to free yourself from the limits and laws of the reasoning mind. Imagining, projects new images on to your mind and changes your approach to a situation. The freedom of imagining will take you into a 'new world' of possibilities.

*Direct Knowing*, is the fourth and final way of

Knowing. There are limits to Knowing via being told, reasoning and imagining as they are born of the human mind. Direct knowing comes from God. How can you have direct knowing? After all, many of you pray to God...... *but does God speak to you?*

By separating illusion from reality, your mind will be open to direct knowing. In this way God will 'speak' to you in every moment, revealing what you really need to know. Whenever you find yourself confused or 'stuck' use the four ways of Knowing to find your way forward.

The Pan Pathway of Relating is the way to master your destiny. With every act of Relating you can take control of your life and prosperity. You will do this by learning and practicing the four stages of Relating - *Meeting, Investigation, Intimacy and Integration.*

*Meeting* is the first stage of Relating. Someone you meet today can be forgotten tomorrow or they could change the direction of your life.

Look how the people you have met are determining your future. Did you meet these people by chance or choice? From the moment you meet, to the last words you speak, every meeting has the potential for you to prosper. Open your mind and make the most of every meeting - opportunity.

*Investigation* is the second stage of Relating. Investigating begins by exploring your true motivation for relating to anything or anyone.

By motivation I mean the desire which moves your relationships. Ask yourself if the desire that moves you stems from fear, pressure, obligation, or to help your Self. If your life is not fulfilling, examine your motivations for relating with your family, friends, food, materials and money.

*Intimacy* is the third stage of Relating. The lack of intimacy is the main cause in the breakdown of all relationships. What is intimacy?

Intimacy is being close physically, mentally, emotionally and spiritually. To be intimate you have to share your innermost feelings, needs and aspirations. Open your heart.

Being intimate with one person is the way to be close with everyone. When this happens, you will feel harmony in every relationship.

*Integration* is the fourth and final stage of Relating. It means to become 'one' in body and spirit, with everything in Nature. Integration is the fusion of your body and spirit with everything you are relating with.

Just as all the colours come together to form a rainbow, everything you are relating with becomes the fusion of human nature with Nature itself. When you become one with Nature, every act of relating will be powered by the force of Nature.

The Pan Pathway of Relating will give you control over human nature. In this way you will take absolute authority of your destiny.

The Pan Pathway of Creating is the way to complete your God given calling. Each one of you was born to bring a unique gift into the world. The Pan Pathway of Creating will guide you via four stages - *Clarity, Perseverance, Endurance and Completion* to the creation of your calling.

*Clarity* is the first step of Creating. Your calling is a life long journey of creating and without clarity of mind, vision and direction, you will get lost on the way.

When you embark upon *any* venture, do it with a clear mind. To clear your mind, separate illusion from reality, then draw from the way of Knowing to attain clarity of direction. If you become lost, stop and reinstate clarity before continuing.

Many of you begin the journey, but few of you complete it, due to your lack of clarity. If your mind is not clear, the journey will never be completed and it may even destroy you.

*Perseverance* is the second step of Creating. On the way, you will encounter unforeseen challenges that arise slowly or suddenly.

Perseverance involves finding ways to overcome every adversity. There will be moments when every way forward appears insurmountable.

Never think of a situation as hopeless. Instead, have faith and persevere. When you step out in faith, the hand of God will move to help you.

*Endurance* is the third step of Creating. This stage can last for a day, a decade or even longer depending on the nature of your calling.

Endurance takes you beyond your limits to the furthest point you have ever been. To keep going when your mind and body wants to quit, you need to exercise your will power. To increase your will power, choose to *be* with God and believe that you will complete your calling.

*Completion* is the fourth and final step of Creating. It means to finish and enjoy what you have created. This sounds easy and yet so many never reach completion. Why? You can create as much as you want, but if it is not in accord with God's will, you will never finish what you were born to create.

To complete your life's calling you have to embark on your God given calling. Only then will you experience the joy of completion.

Each one of you is now facing a unique set of challenges in your life journey. The Pan Pathway of Creating will help you, from idea to completion, to overcome every challenge from baking bread to feeding starving millions. In this way you will complete your God given calling.

In the following Five Lessons, you will learn how to use The Pan Pathways on your life's journey. As you journey on the Pathways, you will need to overcome fear and doubt.

*The Sacred Steps** will help you to overcome your every fear and doubt. Your right foot stands for faith to overcome doubt and your left is for the courage to dispel fear. By applying The Pan Pathways and The Sacred Steps, you will have the trust of a 'tightrope walker' to overcome every impossibility.

* The Sacred Steps: Taken from The HELP Book

# ~ Lesson Two In Practice ~

**Aim:** To exercise your supernatural power. To free yourself in spirit, mind and heart and come alive. To demonstrate your God given power and purpose in every action.

**Method:** The Pan Pathway of Being frees your spirit; Knowing awakens your mind; Relating opens your heart and Creating enables you to complete your God given calling.

**Practice:** Every time you are faced with a challenge, read and reflect on The Pan Pathways again. Then work each pathway into your decisions and actions from idea to completion. By using The Sacred Steps of faith and courage you will overcome every fear and doubt.

**Result:** Every time you practice The Pan Pathways, you will feel the power of God flowing into your spirit, mind, heart and body. When that happens, you will manifest miracles in every action.

~ **Lesson Three** ~

# THE HELP PROCESS

# IN

# PRACTICE

*The HELP Process will help
every human being, in every situation
and in every moment of the day.*
The HELP Book

*The energy, power and authority to work miracles comes when The Foundations of HELP and The Pan Pathways work together as The HELP Process In Practice .......*

The Third Lesson is to learn how to work miracles in your daily life. The word miracle means 'an act of supernatural power' or 'an event due to supernatural agency.' That agency is God.

Many of you believe in God, but do not believe in miracles. Why? Because you do not know how to exercise your God given power and authority to perform miracles.

You are learning to work miracles, but how will *you* actually get the power and authority? After all, even the most powerful and spiritual leaders in your land lack the means to manifest miracles.

I am going to teach you how to work miracles at *will*. The miracles I speak of are not performed by mystical or magical means, but by the power and authority of God.

In this lesson, you will learn how to exercise your God given power and authority to work miracles, via a simple and practical process. We begin with a question:

How does a miracle happen?

When God's will is put into action. God is the agency and you are the agent that puts the will of God into action. Every action is powered by energy and by exercising your power in accordance with God's will, you have the power and authority to work miracles. But how do you do that?

The Foundations of HELP provide you with all your energy and The Pan Pathways channel that energy into every action. Practiced together as The HELP Process they transform all your energy into actions of supernatural power - miracles.

All your energy comes from your Health, Home, Family and Work and by nurturing each, you tap into the very source of your God given power. When that happens you will overflow with power.

The Pan Pathways channel your power into action. Being, Knowing, Relating and Creating channel your power according to God's will. The more your power flows through these pathways, the more powerful your actions will be.

When an action becomes supercharged with power, a supernatural event takes place - a miracle. The energy, power and authority to work miracles comes when The Foundations of HELP and The Pan Pathways work *together* as The HELP Process In Practice.

Are you a believer with energy, who lacks the channel and authority to exercise your power into action? The HELP Process provides you with the energy and channel to use your God given power and authority to work miracles. All this sounds wonderful, even true, but how can you work miracles when managing your life is hard enough? If your life is hard, it is because *you* have forsaken your God given power and authority to work miracles.

A human being is a supernatural creature and creating miracles is your birthright. You have become a supernatural creature as a result of a long line of miraculous events in our evolution.

Your power and authority to perform miracles was demonstrated by one of the most supernatural events in the evolution of our species:

The leap from ape man to the first human.

This evolutionary leap was powered by our ancient ancestors and their ability to make tools. The creative challenge of making and using tools made extraordinary demands on the brain, increasing its use and size.

But what made this leap possible?

To create anything, you must use The Pan

Pathways of Being, Knowing, Relating and Creating. Unbeknown to our ancient ancestors they worked these pathways to create a supernatural event.

How did the first humans make tools?

From their Being they had the idea of tools and with their Knowing they started Relating with stones and sticks. Then by using their skills of Creating they made tools.

Another supernatural event that changed the course of human evolution was the creation of fire. But how did *Homo Erectus* make fire and pass on the process to others?

This is how Stone Age man made fire. From their Being, they had the idea of fire which was coupled with their Knowing about kindling, wood and flint stones. By Relating to these elements with their skills of Creating, they made fire.

Our ancestors used The Pan Pathways, all be it unknowingly to ascend from the animal realm into the human realm. Their creative capacity helped them to hunt, make clothes, shelter and even create works of art.

Every time you use tools or make fire, you too use The Pan Pathways. Every act of creation is the result of the pathways of Being, Knowing, Relating and Creating at work. It is by *working* these pathways that you create.

In fact, everything you have created is a result of The Pan Pathways at work. Choose any activity, object or event you have created and see how you worked your Being, Knowing, Relating and Creating.

Whatever you have chosen has come into Being via the interplay of your Knowing, Relating and Creating. Every process of creation begins and ends with Being.

To understand what I am saying, do your utmost to cancel out any of these pathways that were not present in the process of Creating whatever you have chosen. Also, try to add more pathways that you deem necessary.

You will find that The Pan Pathways govern every action of creation. When you use these pathways, they become channels that transform your power into action.

To show you the power of The Pan Pathways in action, I will use events from my own life. Although all four pathways work in unison, I will demonstrate the power of each pathway to help you live a supernatural existence.

The Pan Pathway of Being is the channel for God to give me the authority to exercise my supernatural power. That is why I have the power and authority to create whatever I wish.

Being focused on the realm of reality, my spirit is free from illusion. Being a free spirit, I live and let God guide my mind, body and soul in every action.

Being guided by God, I have been on time for every meeting and completed every responsibility early since the age of eighteen. Without running from pillar-to-post, everything I need is provided for miraculously: Look, my life is Paradise.

The Pan Pathway of Knowing gives me the wisdom of how to live, what to seek, the words to speak and the way to act. In this way I am the master of my own destiny.

Knowing who I am and my God given purpose, gives me absolute faith. Faith in *my Self* is helping me to continue on an epoch making journey of discovery.

Knowing how to increase my Knowing is the way I have found solutions to overcome every challenge. The ways of Knowing enabled me to create and publish The HELP Books world-wide.

The Pan Pathway of Relating channels my life's work into the world. My *soul* purpose is to help create Pan Paradise on Earth and with every act of Relating I fulfil my life's work.

Relating carries my work like a wave of water that is flowing around the Earth and now it has reached you. In this way I will continue Relating to many Beings now and forever. Relating enables me to give and receive all the love, money and materials needed to support a supernatural existence.

The Pan Pathway of Creating guides me on every step of creating my calling. The vision of diffusing *The HELP Consciousness** was once only a dream of people joining hands around the Earth.

Creating a world-wide programme for the creation of Pan Paradise on Earth without a leader, following, organization, hierarchy or buildings was thought to be impossible. Now it is happening.

The way of Creating is helping me to embark on adventures in human evolution that will change the evolutionary direction of humanity from *hunter-hunted* (competition) to *helper-helped* (co-operation).

Being able to live a supernatural existence is based on my ability to practice The HELP Process with mastery. My aim is to show you how The HELP Process is practiced to work supernatural events in your daily life.

* The HELP Consciousness: Pioneered by Raja

The interaction of help is governed by a process that can be learned, taught and practiced with absolute mastery. This process will change your understanding and use of the activity of help *forever*.

How does the process of HELP actually work?

Every interaction of help is powered by the energy from your Health, Home, Family and Work, channelled by your Being, Knowing, Relating and Creating into action.

By using the resources from your foundations, via the pathways, to nurture your Health, Home, Family and Work, your potential to help yourself will continue to increase. The more help you are capable of giving and receiving, the more you will create what you need, dream and desire.

This is called The HELP Process because it works to help you in every situation. The HELP Process is a phenomenal discovery because it actually increases your capacity to give and receive help at your point of need.

So far, humans have used elements of The HELP Process without knowing how they work or understanding their full potential. By learning how to use The Pan Pathways to nurture, The Foundations of HELP, you will help yourself in every action.

Before the discovery of The HELP Process, humans struggled to help themselves survive and procreate. Now, each one of you can give and receive all the help you need to overcome every challenge and create the supernatural.

For the first time in our evolution the process of HELP can be used *consciously* to increase our capacity to help each other. The more we help each other to develop our foundations of life, the more we promote Human Evolution and Life Procreation.

The HELP Process is a sacred science that governs every action and interaction in creation. This process is being taught in education as the universal process for developing human potential.

The Discovery of The HELP Process marks the beginning of a new epoch in our evolution, as it will accelerate co-operation in every field of human endeavour. In this way The HELP process will change the evolutionary direction of humanity from competition to co-operation.

In the next four lessons, we shall explore the practice and potential of The HELP Process. Once you have learned The HELP Process In Practice, you will use it at will to manage every situation and manifest the supernatural.

# ~ Lesson Three In Practice ~

**Aim:** To Exercise your God given power and authority to work supernatural events - miracles in your daily life.

**Method:** Use The HELP Process - The Pan Pathways of Being, Knowing, Relating and Creating to improve and empower your foundations of life. By repeating this process your energy - capacity will increase to manifest actions of supernatural power.

**Practice:** First, you need to be still - silent each day and focus on a challenge you have in your Health, Home, Family and Work. Then, read and work The Pan Pathways to change your current situation and create new conditions.

**Result:** As you practice The HELP Process each day, the power of God will flow through The Pan Pathways into your actions. In this way miracles will manifest in your Health, Home, Family and Work.

~ **Lesson Four** ~

# HELP FOR YOUR

# HEALTH

*The whole person needs to be*
*nurtured in order to be healthy.*
The HELP Book

*The purpose of health*
*is to live in a pure condition of being.*
*Being is the epitome of health* . . . . . . .

The Fourth Lesson is to learn how to empower your foundation of Health. Being healthy is your primal responsibility and first priority in life.

Each one of you has descended from a long line of ancestors. First the ape-like man and his successors the nomad and hunters, the early settlers, then finally came your descendants, and now you.

Human health is the unbroken stream of life that has sustained the evolutionary journey of our species from the dawn of creation. Human health contains the lineage of our supernatural powers.

Without The Foundation of Health, humans would have become extinct. Health provided our ancient ancestors with the energy to survive and procreate despite extreme conditions. Yet today, so many of you have barely enough energy to make it through the day. Why?

Your Health is your primary source of energy.

Like a battery that powers a radio, your health powers your life. Just as a dead battery cannot power a radio, poor health will make you powerless - lifeless.

In this lesson I will teach you how to harness the miraculous powers of your health. I do not mean the kind of health peddled by the latest fads and fashions. After all, many people spend continually on the quest for health but remain powerless.

I am going to show you how to increase your energy by *empowering* your health. You may have heard of ultra health, perfect health, ideal health and so on, but what does it mean to empower your health? Empower means: to endow with power, electrify, switch on, strengthen, magnetize or enable.

A human body is a complex web of energy that is used to perform actions in order to sustain itself. Every action needs energy which comes from your health. By empowering your health, you increase your energy.

How do you empower your Health?

The Foundation of Health is the primary source of your energy. The Pan Pathways channel the energy you have at this moment into actions that nurture - empower your health.

In this way, The HELP Process creates a cycle of energy - action - energy, to increase the power of your health. Our aim is to use The Pan Pathways to empower your health in every action.

We begin with The Pathway of Being by separating illusion from reality concerning your health, habits, motivations and goals. Your Being contains the perfect picture of your health, but the illusions have blurred your vision.

What is your vision of health? Starting with your goals, ask yourself whether or not they are born of illusion. Are you focused on goals for your health set forth by society or your Self?

What is the goal of health?

Is health for its own sake or does it serve a higher purpose? Many of you spend a lot of time, money and effort trying to attain 'perfect health' without ever reaching your goal.

One of the most illusory goals peddled by the media, is via the marketing of products that make you feel good. These can range from alcohol and drugs to beauty and health treatments.

There are countless products on the market that claim to make you feel good. In reality they set illusory goals for you to follow. The goals you have chosen for your health determine the condition of your wellbeing.

The word wellbeing, is often used in the development of health, but what does it mean?

Some of you have made wellbeing your goal and yet continue to struggle with your health. Why?

Wellbeing can only be realized when your life is based on Being. It is the *being* in wellbeing that is the real goal of health. After all, many people feel well, without 'being.'

What is the condition of your Being?

The purpose of The Foundation of Health is to live in a pure condition of being. Being is the epitome of Health. Your Being is the centre of your existence and guides all the events in your life.

Being is the meaning and purpose of your life. By 'being itself' you free your spirit to follow your Self. When that happens, you become Self-motivated and Self-empowered.

The Pathway of Knowing will help you to know your motivations in the development of your Foundation of Health. I want you to question your motivation for developing your health.

Being true to your health is about knowing what

motivates your choices and actions. Health is not a chance it is a choice. Knowing how to make choices that nurture your health is the key to wellbeing.

Everyday you make thousands of choices that affect your health - body, mind and emotions. The current condition of your health is the story of your choices and actions.

Have you been true to your health?

What drives most people to abuse their health are bad habits and the pressure to conform to public expectations. The way you live or your 'life-style' determines your Health.

Is your lifestyle helping or harming your health? Look at what you eat and drink, the things you buy, the clothes you wear and the way you behave in public. Are you free to do as you please or a slave to your conditioning and lifestyle?

Your style makes you feel self-conscious in public and forces you to put on a show. The more self-conscious you are, the more you will adopt a lifestyle to gain acceptance and avoid rejection. Does that ring true? When you were a baby, you did not have a lifestyle - that is why you were healthy. The beauty and power of being human radiated from your body and as you played naked, your parents looked at you in awe.

In knowing the motivations behind your choices, you will start finding and fulfilling your real needs again. Then all your choices, from the shoes on your feet to the words you speak, will be true to your Being.

By being true to your health, more and more of your real needs will be met. When this happens all your bad habits and fears of public opinion will fall away like dead leaves in Autumn.

Every choice will become an opportunity for you to help and heal the aches and pains in your body, mind and emotions.

Knowing how to heal your health will enable you to heal others. Look how I am using my knowing to help, heal and empower your health and that of everyone I relate with.

The Pathway of Relating will help you to empower your health in ways you did not think possible. Everything that surrounds you is helping you to stay alive and by relating fully with your surroundings you empower your health.

At this moment your health is being sustained by relating to the elements, materials and microbes. The way you relate with your environment determines the condition of your health.

Every act of relating either helps or harms your health. An act of help is a healing experience which energizes your body. Even the smallest action of help makes you feel better. Why?

Help contains miraculous powers to heal.

Helping yourself and others, releases the indwelling spirit of God and generates love in your body. The feelings of love energize every part of the body, from the bone marrow to the brain cells.

Love has been as powerful a healer in our evolution as medicine. For millions of years, our ancestors have survived cuts, bruises, wounds, infections, diseases and plagues by helping each other. From the laying on of hands, to brain surgery, humans have relied on each other to reinstate health.

The activity of helping is the key to healing.

The first thing you do when someone is ill or hurt is to get help. If you have ever been seriously ill, then every act of help, from yourself, your family, friends and doctors healed you.

Whatever challenges you face in your health, *giving and receiving help* is the only way you will overcome them. Some of the most fatal injuries and diseases have been cured simply by people helping each other.

Relating via giving and receiving help, in every action, will enable you to help yourself create your vision of health. How healthy do you wish to be?

The Pathway of Creating will guide you in the

creation of supernatural health. When God first breathed life into humans, our health became the source imbued with miraculous power.

The Foundation of Health is the source of miraculous energy that has enabled humans to create works of music, art, architecture, technology, medicine and so on, over the past three million years.

Our aim then, is to harness our God given power of health to live a supernatural existence. But how do we do that? Simple - by finding and fulfilling the real needs of our health: body, mind, emotion and spirit.

Be quiet, and listen to the real needs coming from your health. Once you have found a need, focus your energy on fulfilling it completely. If you find a need that you cannot fulfil yourself, then seek advice and get help.

With every real need you fulfil, you will increase your energy - power to fulfil more needs. The constant fulfilment of your real needs will energize your health with supernatural power.

Creating your Foundation of Health, is your primal responsibility in life, because your Home, Family and Work are dependent on you. What you desire to create with your life will depend on the condition of your health.

The more you are called to create with your life, the more you will need to empower your Foundation of Health. Look back at your health and see how much it has shaped your existence.

What have you created with your life?

Look how the supernatural power of my Foundation of Health is helping me to manifest a world-wide programme for the creation of Pan Paradise on Earth.

By empowering your health, you will have the energy to create a supernatural existence. You see, your body, mind, emotions and spirit is endowed with the collective qualities of countless generations.

You are a supernatural Being.

You have a mind that can understand truth, goodness, beauty and being - a body with the strength to climb mountains, cross deserts and oceans - emotions that can feel the compassion of a saint and a spirit that contains the courage, faith, love and joy of God.

In your Health dwells a supernatural Being.

I want you to awaken that Being, by empowering your health. It is because you do not know how to empower your health, that you are powerless. Many of you strongly desire to change society, but cannot make it happen. Why? Because you are weak.

Wake up. From here on in, start thinking of Health as your real source of power. Do whatever it takes to put your health first. Be still, be silent and be focused on nurturing your real needs. You have a choice - either to waste your health or use it to shine as brightly as a supernova.

## ~ Lesson Four In Practice ~

**Aim:** To empower your Foundation of Health. To harness the miraculous power of your health and create a supernatural existence.

**Method:** The Foundation of Health is the primary source of all your energy. The Pan Pathways channel your energy into actions that nurture your health. That is how The HELP Process recycles all your energy into actions that empower your health.

**Practice:** Use every situation and action as an opportunity to serve the real needs of your health. Listen to your body, mind, emotions and spirit. If in doubt ask your Self: Is this what I really need for my health to thrive and prosper?

**Result:** The HELP Process will activate an 'energy-action-energy' loop, that will empower your health perpetually. Your health will then become energized with supernatural power, enabling you to achieve all that you need, dream and desire.

~ Lesson Five ~

# HELP FOR YOUR

# HOME

*Our home is a*
*reflection of the Self.*
The HELP Book

*The way you relate with the people*
*and possessions in your home determine*
*the power, prosperity and love in your life* .......

The Fifth Lesson is to learn how to empower your Home. Your dwelling place is your home and the cornerstone of your life.

Humans are one of the most fragile and vulnerable creatures on the Earth. The Home has helped our species to survive and thrive for over three million years.

The home you live in has evolved from the days when primitive man needed protection, against physical danger from fellow man, wild animals and hazardous weather.

The home base enabled our ancestors to *manage* the most extreme conditions, ranging from animal attacks to surviving ice ages.

The cave was a natural abode for our ancient ancestors. There they were less vulnerable and found some protection, dry conditions and warmth. Man as a cave dweller occupied many parts of the world for many generations.

Despite popular belief, early humans did not *start out* as cave men. The earliest archeological finds reveal that primitive man may have lived exclusively in the open. This does not mean that the first humans were 'homeless' creatures.

One of the oldest sites where stone implements have been found *(Olduvai in East Africa)* shows an artificially formed boundary of bones. The first homes made by man could well have been small enclosures - windbreakers, constructed from stones, bones and branches.

The next phase in evolution took place when

humans gathered in groups of families on the edge of water ways where they fished, or in river valleys where they grew corn. At this point, humans were forced to make dwellings - huts of grass, boughs of trees, mud bricks and stones appeared.

As time passed, such groups became larger and their dwellings became more permanent and solid in structure. The hamlet led to the village, the town and finally the vast modern and complex city.

Today, our essentials still include the basic needs of primitive man to which has been added the requirements of the Modern Age.

The evolution of the human home is about to take another quantum leap with the discovery of The Foundations of HELP. The Home is as much a foundation of human existence as your Health, Family and Work.

Your Home is a tool for life-management.

As discussed in The HELP Book, your Home is your primary 'tool' which you use to manage your

Health, Family and Work. Just as a bad tool will bodge up the job, a bad home will mess up your life. Are you with me?

In this lesson you will learn how to manage the miraculous potential of your home. The home I speak of is not the kind you see in movies, magazines and exhibitions. After all, many of you are very house proud, but your lives are a mess.

I am going to show you how to create a supernatural home and harness its energy to empower your life. Every action you perform uses energy and home is where you go to rest and recharge your energy - power. By empowering your home, you increase your energy.

How do you empower your Home?

By using The Pan Pathways of Being, Knowing, Relating and Creating to channel the energy from your Health, Family and Work to renew your Home. My aim is to help you to create a home that enables you to live a supernatural existence.

Starting with The Pathway of Being, separate illusion and reality regarding your needs, dreams and desires for your home. Your Being contains the blue print of the kind of home you need now, but the illusions are misleading you. Ask yourself:

What is the real purpose of my home?

Is your dwelling place purely a material possession or can it support a spiritual purpose? A lot of people invest most of their energy and resources building a 'dream home', but the wish of a dream home remains just that, a dream.

Your dream of a home may be fine, but are your wishes in line with the your real needs? The home you live in is either a place for your Self or your ego. If your mind is following the realm of illusion, then your ego is in control of your home.

When a home is ruled by the ego, every action is motivated to serve illusory needs, dreams and desires. So how do you know if your home is run to *inflate* the ego or *serve* the needs of being human?

The Pathway of Knowing will reveal the true motivations in your home life. To find out some 'home truths', separate all the belongings that actually serve your real needs, from those that do not. Be honest with yourself.

Ask yourself: Are you a victim of a home you've filled with hand-me-downs, show piece objects and stores of foods and goods? How much of what you have in your home do you really need to live a supernatural existence?

I want you to simplify your home life by having only that which you need to meet your physical and spiritual needs. Bringing your home life down to the need level sounds like hardship, but letting go of what you do not need is really easy and enjoyable.

What you *actually* need and want are in truth exactly the same and so you are only letting go of what you do not need. By knowing what you need, no one can give you what you do not need.

Everything you have in your home either helps

or harms you. By having only what you need to fulfil your physical and spiritual needs, you will live in harmony in your inner and outer life.

Before you bring anything into your home, you must understand that your possessions make you powerful or powerless. The most important home truth you need to know, is that unnecessary possessions are unnecessary burdens.

Is your home a warehouse or powerhouse?

What you do not need will drain your power and what you do need will make you powerful. A home that does not serve your needs will drain your energy before you leave the front door.

The Pathway of Relating will help you to transform the energy of your home into actions of supernatural power. Just as your health - body is a web of energy, your home is an extension of your energy field.

Your home is your power - house. All the energy, money and materials of your life are kept in your home. In turn, your Health, Family and Work are powered by the energy from your Home.

Every person and possession in your home emits energy which enters your energy field. Energy is either positive or negative. Positive energy will make you power-full and negative energy will make you power-less.

The energy = power equation is very simple. The more positive energy you have in your Home, the more power you have to sustain your Health, Family and Work. The way you relate with the people and possessions in your home determine the power, prosperity and love in your life.

Having people or possessions you do not need in your home, is like putting stones in your shoes that give you grief. Even the most capable people are often crippled by the grief in their homes.

When there is a lack of happiness, people buy products to fill the void. That is why most homes are filled with *things*. How much of what you have in your home, do you *really* need in order to be happy? What you have in your home portrays your aims in life. Your home is a reflection of your Self.

A home is a refuge and a place you feel at peace and ease. Home is also a sacred place and referred to as the 'temple' or 'house of God'.

Your home is where you belong and run to in times of trouble and ill health. It is the place you come to after long journeys, for celebrations, marriages, and giving thanks. That is why we say 'homecoming' or 'home is where the heart is'.

The place you live in is the centre of your life.

It is in your home that you and your family begin and end each day. The Foundation of Home is the cornerstone of your existence. To live a supernatural existence, you need to create a home that contains supernatural power.

How do you create a supernatural home?

The Pathway of Creating will guide you in the making of a supernatural home that will change the place you live into an oracle of energy.

We begin by building on the fact that every object in your home is emitting energy. All the objects in turn create a web of energy which interacts with your body.

Every-body is a source of energy and by interacting with objects that increase your energy you create an oracle - web of power that magnetizes your home.

By choosing objects that emit supernatural power and placing them in your home, you will activate what I call *The Pan Life Manifestation Process.*\* This process works via the use of eight objects and symbols that empower - magnetize your home and help you to attract what you need.

A symbol is both physical and non physical in nature, just like a human being. Symbols represent your inner and outer reality and are a point of unity between your inner and outer world. Objects such as a pen, cup, candle or lamp are potential symbols.

\* The Pan Life Manifestation Process. Taken from The HELP Book

I want you to choose eight symbolic objects. Choose four that represent your Health, Home Family and Work and four that represent your Being, Knowing, Relating and Creating. Then place these objects carefully in the following positions in and around your home. From the centre of your home place the symbol for:

- *Knowing at the front door (12 o'clock)*
- *Being at the back (6 o'clock)*
- *Relating to the right (3 o'clock)*
- *Creating to the left (9 o'clock)*

*In between, place the symbol for Family at two o'clock, Health at four o'clock, Home at eight o'clock and Work at ten o'clock. Are you with me so far?*

Once the symbols are placed, *The Pan Life Personal Oracle* is activated. Each day focus your thoughts and emotions on each object to attract what you need in that Foundation or Pathway.

The placement of symbolic objects connects

your subconscious with the outside world. Symbolic objects become activated by strong thoughts and emotions which then manifest as physical objects, conditions or events in your life. When the symbols you have placed reach a certain intensity, they become supercharged - magnetized and attract whatever you are focused on with that symbol.

The intensity of your thoughts and emotions on the symbolic objects is vital in the process of physical materialisation.

The purpose of The Pan Life Manifestation Process is to empower your home with supernatural power. To empower also means to charge, electrify, switch on and magnetize.

The Pan Life Personal Oracle will supercharge your home into a magnetic energy field that will draw everything you need, dream and desire from all spheres. When that happens, your home will attract all the resources you need to sustain and manage a supernatural existence.

# ~ Lesson Five In Practice ~

**Aim:** To empower your Foundation of Home with miraculous energy - power. To create a home that enables you to live a supernatural existence.

**Method:** The Foundation of Home is your power - house of energy. The Pan Pathways transform that energy into actions that empower your Health, Family and Work. Use your Foundation of Home as a tool to manage your life.

**Practice:** Use The Pan Pathways to channel the energy - resources from the other Foundations of HELP - Health, Family and Work to improve your Home. Organize your home life by having only the people and possessions you really need to be happy. Then activate The Pan Life Personal Oracle.

**Result:** Constant practice of The HELP Process *with* The Pan Life Personal Oracle, will intensify the energy field until it reaches a critical mass. Your home will then be magnetized with miraculous power.

# HELP FOR YOUR

# FAMILY

*Our family
is the primary source
of help and love.*
The HELP Book

*The story of the human family is based on help - love. Help and love will enable your family to overcome every crisis and prosper beyond your imagination* .......

The Sixth Lesson is to learn how to empower your Family. Your family is the primary source of love and help in your life.

Each one of you was 'helpless' at birth and your family was the primary source of help and love. In the same way, every successive generation of humans has been helped to survive and procreate by the human family.

The definition of family is, 'a group of related people' or 'descendents of common ancestors.' The family of humans has evolved over the ages, to hunt, farm, build and spread across the Earth.

The human family is the tree of humanity and its roots stem from the dawn of creation. Is it any wonder that in most Faiths, the family has been at the heart of the 'Creation Story.'

Although the evolution of our species can be traced back some five million years, when did the first human family come into existence?

One of the most moving discoveries in human evolution is that of the set of footprints found at *Laetoli* in Tanzania by Mary Leakey.*

In her own words, "....... *a trail left by three people who walked across a flat expanse of volcanic ash three and a half million years ago.......*

*This was a group of people, walking together. One assumes they were perhaps holding hands. They are so evenly spaced....... the tracks and they are keeping step, always left foot for left foot and right foot for right, that it may for all we know........ been a family party."* **

\* Mary Leakey: World renown British Paleoanthropologist.
\*\* Extract from the UK Channel Four Television series: 'Great Excavations.' April 2000.

Another revealing archeological find that points to the evidence of the earliest 'family group' was discovered at *Hadar,* again in Tanzania. Don Johanson* in 1974 found the remains of thirteen *(Australopithecus Afarensis)* individuals who were buried together by a flash flood. He called them the 'first family.'

The 'first family' yielded vital clues in their physical and social structure. The human family was born out of the necessity to survive and procreate in a very challenging environment some 3.2 million years ago.

The family group as a unit, emerged to help itself hunt, safeguard its offspring and care for the sick and crippled. All this implies that emotional relationships - love, must have played a very important part in their lives.

Over the ages, groups became extended families, tribes and races, but the lineage of the family of humans has the same origin and purpose.

* Donald Johanson, Anthropologist. President: Institute of Human Origin, Berkeley, CA, USA.

With help and love, our species has overcome every evolutionary challenge and created miraculous works, inventions and discoveries. Today, the human family is undergoing major changes, but the purpose still remains the same.

So far, the family group has evolved to take care of its own kith and kin. However, with high speed travel and multiracial communities, individuals are finding themselves without the help and love of a family.

To manage the present challenge, a new kind of family group will evolve to include individuals from different biological families. The new family will be 'HELP Groups'* where individuals come together to help and love each other.

In this lesson, you will learn how to create and manage the miraculous power of your family. According to The HELP Consciousness your Family is a source of miraculous man-power that you use to manage your Health, Home and Work.

* HELP Groups, as mentioned in The HELP Book.

I will show you how to empower your family into a supernatural 'unit' and use its energy in the empowerment of your life. Just as a 'bad' team will bungle a project, a 'broken' family will wreck your whole life.

How do you empower your Family?

Channel the energy and resources from your Health, Home, and Work into your Family via The Pan Pathways of Being, Knowing, Relating, and Creating. My aim is to teach you to create a family - HELP Group, that overflows with help and love.

Starting with The Pathway of Being, focus on the realm of reality as the guiding light for your family. Why? Many of you are trying desperately to create an 'ideal family', but the illusions are resulting in conflict and disunity.

What is the real function of a family?

Is your family functioning to amass more and more to serve the illusions - ego, or does it have a higher purpose to help and love each other?

Which realm rules your family, that of reality or illusion? If your family is ruled by the realm of illusion, there will be disharmony and lovelessness. You may have the best money can buy for your family, but a family ruled by the illusions - ego will be a living hell.

Every family, depends on one or more of its members to be the guiding light. If you are that person in your family, then by being true to the realm of reality, you will demonstrate what it means to help and love.

A family without a guiding light, is a family without faith, hope and love. Most of you already know that love is the key to a happy family, but do you know the way to love?

Your Being contains the way to love and the power, wisdom and grace of The Infinite Being - God. The Pathway of Being will enable you to become aware of your blessings and share them with your family.

The Pathway of Knowing will enlighten your mind with a new understanding of love.

The HELP Book states: *"love is not an idea, song, action or a solution. Love is a feeling created via an act of help. Without help, there is no love."*

When we help ourselves and each other, we create feelings of love for everyone. These feelings of love are what we want most from life.

Many people are unhappy with their 'lot', not because they do not have enough, but because of the lack of love in their hearts. Not knowing the way to create love drives them constantly to pursue more things and thrills in the hope of finding love.

One only looks for something that is lost.

Let me tell you the secret of finding love. You cannot find love. Love is what you feel now. Help is the way to feel love.

Every action you perform, either helps or harms your Self, other people and the Earth. To harm is to hurt. To help is to love. But, how do you know which actions are harmful and change them to be helpful actions?

An action that is motivated by the realm of illusion will lead to domination and disharmony. Actions born of the realm of reality will result in freedom and love. By knowing the motivation behind your actions, you will know when your actions are harmful or helpful.

Knowing the way to separate your motivations from illusion to reality, will enable you to perform actions that increase - generate feelings of love, in your family, with your friends and your community.

The Pathway of Relating will help you to give and receive all the help you need to empower your family. In the same way your Foundation of Health is a supernatural source of energy, your Family is an omnipotent source of help.

Every person in your family is a part of a dynamic unit that thrives by helping each other. Just as the 'first family' emerged naturally to help each other, the interaction of help is pivotal in the empowerment of your family.

Helping each other makes our lives easier, more comfortable and prosperous. Common sense tells us that the more we help each other, the more powerful our families will become.

By relating, to give and receive help, you activate the most powerful force in the world, the power of love. Every act of help will generate love and the more you give and receive help, the more love will empower your family.

Giving and receiving help is the only way to empower your family with love. An abundance of love will transform your family into an omnipotent force. At this point, the family you live in will attract everything it needs to help itself.

Many families are living in fear and lack, not because there is not enough, but as a result of not helping each other. Even the most spiritual families often do not have the time, money and energy to help others. No matter how poor or hopeless the prospects for your family may be, giving and receiving help will turn every adversity into an opportunity for prosperity.

When people help each other miracles happen.

The story of the human family is based on help and love. Help and love will enable your family to overcome every crisis and prosper beyond your imagination. There are no limits to what your family can create.

The Pathway of Creating will guide you in the empowerment of a family that will be able to manifest superabundantly.

How do you create a superabundant Family?

By building on the understanding that helping each other generates the most powerful force in creation - love. Our aim is to exercise the power of love to manifest miracles.

Many of you have read and heard a lot about love. The world is full of wise men and women who teach and preach about love, but where are the families that demonstrate, exercise and manifest the miraculous?

My family, is a HELP group of a handful of people. We are manifesting the miraculous by diffusing The HELP Consciousness world-wide. We do not have a leader, following, organization or hierarchy and yet we send these books to thousands of people around the world as *gifts*.

How will your family manifest the miraculous?

Simple - by giving according to the will of God. When you give according to the will of God, you plant seeds in the most fertile ground. These seeds grow, multiply and come back to you.

One act of giving, grows a hundred fold and returns to the giver. What you give you will receive and by giving you will in turn be given much more.

Is your family living superabundantly?

If not, it is because you are not letting God guide your giving of time, money, energy and materials. Simple as it sounds, all the lack in your family is caused by holding on and miss - giving what God has blessed you with. The way to give freely is by asking God to guide your giving.

Let go and let God control your giving.

Every act of help is an act of giving and when you give according to God's will, your giving helps the receiver in full. The fullness of giving and receiving results in the fullness of love. The fullness of love in your family will then overflow into the world via giving.

Giving and receiving help is the way to love. That is why for over two decades I have not said 'I love you' to anyone, yet my family life continues to increase superabundantly. How?

I give everything, as though it belongs to God.

Giving according to the will of God mobilizes the miraculous power of love, which comes back to you in the form of blessings. In this way your family life will be blessed superabundantly.

## ~ Lesson Six In Practice ~

**Aim:** To empower your Family with the love of God. To create a family that can give and receive all the help it needs to live superabundantly.

**Method:** Use The Pan Pathways of Being, Knowing, Relating and Creating to channel the energy from your Health, Home, and Work to help each other in your Family. Apply The HELP Process to increase the interaction of help.

**Practice:** Introduce The HELP Process to your family. If you do not have a biological family, establish a HELP Group of like-minded people. Look for opportunities to help each other and practice giving and receiving freely. Let go and let God control your giving.

**Result:** Increasing the capacity to give and receive help will transform your family into a miraculous source of love. When that happens, your family will manifest superabundantly.

# ~ Lesson Seven ~

# HELP FOR YOUR

# WORK

*Working to help others
is the ultimate contribution
we can make to humanity.*
The HELP Book

*To work for another is to be a slave,*
*to work for God is to be free* . . . . . . .

The Seventh Lesson is to learn how to empower your Work. Work is your primary source of livelihood and your central calling in life.

Work is a universal activity that drives the human world culture. Wherever you go, work is foremost on people's mind.

Why is the quest for work so powerful?

The work that you do, helps to provide for yourself and your family. Without work, your livelihood would cease, causing a threat to your existence. Survival is the first law of life and work has helped to sustain our existence since the genesis of human evolution. Being able to work, enabled humans to survive, multiply and now become 'masters of the Earth.' All the things we have created are the result of our handiwork.

Indeed, the word human means *handyman*. But why and how did the activity of work actually begin? After all, other creatures have survived and thrived without having to work as humans have.

The first evidence of human handiwork was the making of stone tools by our ancient ancestors. The use of flint stones was common as it has the best cutting edge. They quarried and made these into tools, usually at the same place.

Archeologists call these places 'Flint Stations' as this is where ancient people, sat down and made the flint stones into tools.

Were the 'Flint Stations' the first 'work sites' and the origin of work as we know it? Or did real work, steady work, labour for one's livelihood, come into being with the advent of agriculture?

Over the ages, the nature of work has changed, but the struggle to provide for one's livelihood has become worse. Unlike our ancient ancestors who could hunt and gather, today over a billion human beings cannot work, even for food.

With the discovery of The HELP Process, human work will evolve to provide supernaturally for what I call a *Pan Human* * existence. Just as *homo hablis* became *homo erectus* in our past, in the future humans will evolve into Pan Humans who will exist in superabundance, working together as one family.

In this lesson you will learn how to harness the miraculous power of work and use it to create and provide for a supernatural existence. Not to do the work common to so many, but to do the kind of work that empowers generations to come.

How do you empower your work?

By learning the way to work The Pan Pathways of Being, Knowing, Relating and Creating. This will

* Pan Human: Meaning whole human. Taken from The HELP Book

provide all the resources you need to project your God given calling into the world.

We begin with The Pathway of Being, which will guide you to do your work. To work is to do and your Being will guide you - not to 'overdo' or 'underdo' anything.

The dictionary gives as its first definition of *being* the word *existence*. Your work determines the condition of your existence - being.

Being comes before doing. Why?

Doing without being is the cause of all the business and laziness in our world. The absence of being drives people to 'overdo' and be busy or 'underdo' and be lazy. Anyone who is busy or lazy is not being guided by their Being.

How can you live and work in accordance with your Being? By changing your motivation for work from the realm of illusion to reality.

If you are motivated by the realm of illusion, your employer is the ego. When you are guided by the realm of reality you work for God.

Who do you work for - your ego or God?

So many of you work yourselves to the bone, not knowing why you never have enough to provide for yourself or your family. Is your employer not paying you enough or are you not doing the most rewarding kind of work?

The Pathway of Knowing will show you how to work for God. The HELP Consciousness states that no one shall work for another but God. To work for another is to be a slave. To work for God is to be free.

You begin by asking God to reveal your vision of work. Your vision is the purpose of your work and payment is the provision to make it happen. When God gives you a vision - work, you will always have the provision - payment to fulfil it.

I have heard many people talk about their visions, but the bottom line is very often an excuse. *"I don't have enough money, time, people, energy...."* Why?

Is your vision from the ego or God?

Who you work for and the kind of work you do, will determine whether you live in lack or superabundance. Even the wisest and the wealthiest amongst you often do not have the provision to manifest your vision.

Do you really think God is stupid enough to give you a vision without the provision to make it happen? I remember when I was a boy, my mother used to send me to buy bread. She always gave me more than enough money.

Every God given vision comes with the provision to make it happen. In one vision God asked me, *"to create The HELP Book and distribute 120 million copies, in one hundred and twenty nations, during the next forty years, without an organization."*

That seems impossible. Well, God has always asked me to do the impossible. Doing the impossible, means that I live superabundantly which requires faith in God.

Many of you have lofty visions, but do not have the provisions to make them manifest. Why? Either your vision is born of your ego or you are not acting with faith.

The Pathway of Relating will enable you to act with faith and courage, by relating with God directly. The HELP Consciousness is not a religion but a direct relationship with God.

By relating with God directly, the power of God will make you act with faith and courage. I call these *The Sacred Steps*\* because they are used in your walk with God. Your right foot stands for *faith* and your left foot stands for *courage*.

No matter how impossible your vision, The Sacred Steps will make it possible. The way to walk The Sacred Steps is by asking God to give you a vision - work.

Then thank God for your vision, before you receive it. That demonstrates your faith in God. Once you know your vision, start preparing to make

\* The Sacred Steps: As explained in The HELP Book

it happen, which requires faith and courage.

Faith will give you hope to overcome doubt and courage will take you out of your 'comfort zone' into the unknown. The Sacred Steps awaken your natural faith and courage, the faith and courage you were born with. They will empower and enhance your relationship with God.

The more you relate with God, the more your faith and courage will increase to help manifest your vision. Faith and courage are like muscles that grow stronger with exercise. As your faith and courage grows stronger, God will give you bigger visions.

The Pathway of Creating will guide you to create your God given vision - work which will provide superabundantly for you and your family as well as for future generations.

The purpose of creating your vision is not only to have enough for yourself and your family, but also to provide for others. A God given vision is always a part of a much bigger picture.

A lot of spiritual people are not able to create their God given vision, because they are living in the 'natural' for themselves. To create a vision, you have to move from the 'natural' into the 'supernatural.' But how do you do that?

Simply by doing exactly as God asks of you. Building on The Sacred Steps, our aim now is to *act* with faith and courage. Everything you do is either born of fear and cowardice or faith and courage.

Fear and cowardice will keep you in the natural, whereas faith and courage takes you into the supernatural. *You cannot live in the natural and create the supernatural.*

You will learn how to create a supernatural existence by acting with faith and courage. Although everything you do can be seen as actions, The HELP Consciousness defines all your actions - human actions as *words and works.*

By exercising your words and works with faith and courage, your actions become supernatural. The most powerful words and works are those that help.

To help is to give and one act of giving comes back to the giver one hundred fold. That is why my books will never become best *sellers*, because God has asked me to give them as *gifts*. Anyone who sells anything, has yet to evolve their words and works to the divine act of giving.

Words and works that are powered by faith and courage, become supernatural actions which yield to provide superabundantly for the creation of your God given vision.

At sixteen years of age I heard my calling to help humanity create Pan Paradise on Earth. Look how my words and works are spreading The HELP Consciousness across the Earth. By exercising your words and works with faith and courage, you too will create your God given vision.

# ~ Lesson Seven In Practice ~

**Aim:** To empower your Foundation of Work. To harness the miraculous power of your work and provide superabundantly for your livelihood.

**Method:** Work The Pan Pathways of Being, Knowing, Relating and Creating to channel your words and works into supernatural actions. Use The Sacred Steps to move from the 'natural' into the 'supernatural.'

**Practice:** Pray and ask God to reveal your vision - work. Then work and walk The Sacred Steps of faith and courage to empower your words and works. Keep praying and believing in your Self to complete your vision. Expect miracles.

**Result:** By exercising your words and works with faith and courage, your actions will become supernatural. When that happens, your words and works will yield superabundantly, to provide for a supernatural existence.

# HELPING YOUR-SELF

*The ultimate act of helping yourself,*
*is to devote your Self to God.*

O nce you have read this book, your ability to help yourself will have increased many fold. As you put The Seven Lessons of **How To HELP Your-*Self*** into practice, you will be able to help yourself in every aspect of your life.

The more you practice The HELP Process, the more you will be able to help your Self. In this way you will develop your responsibility to fulfil all your needs, dreams and desires.

What does that mean? Helping yourself is about taking the responsibility to fulfil all your needs, dreams and desires. The word responsibility stands for your *ability* to *respond*. Helping yourself then, requires you to develop your Self - response - ability.

The First Level of Self-responsibility is the fulfilment of your own needs. From the moment of your birth, every cry was motivated by the need to fulfil your needs for food, warmth and affection.

As you grew, the means of responding to your needs became more and more complex. You began to use tools, such as a spoon to feed yourself, toys to develop your dexterity and gestures to get what you needed.

Since then, you have learned countless skills, to fulfil your ever increasing needs. Look at your ability to use language, machinery and computers as well as scientific and spiritual principles.

You have learned many skills to help you live your life. But, have you managed to fulfil *all* your needs? If not, then you have not yet fulfilled your primary responsibility - helping your Self.

Many of you have had the best education and training money can buy, yet your very needs of being human are crying out to you. Why? Because you do not know how to *give and receive* help.

Helping yourself necessitates that you ask others to help you and for you to help in response. Whatever you need in your life will be fulfilled by helping others. Helping yourself means giving and receiving help - love.

You may be a very independent, wealthy, wise and competent man or woman, but if *all* your needs are not met, you will need to increase your capacity to give and receive help. Only then will you have fulfilled your primary responsibility to help yourself.

The Second Level of Self-responsibility is having the ability to create your dreams. Almost everyone has a dream they want to realize. But how many of you actually manage to make your dreams come true? A lot of people have lofty dreams and visions, but they often remain just that - dreams.

How can you make your dreams come true?

Whereas the fulfilment of your needs requires *natural* ability, a dream demands *supernatural* response - ability to help yourself.

The way to make your dreams come true is by increasing your ability to give and receive help. Look at any figure in our past whose dream has come to be and you will see how much help was given and received in its creation.

Since I was a boy, I have had a recurring dream of people joining hands around the Earth. My dream is for humans to help each other to create Pan Paradise on Earth. Now, day by day, my dream is coming true. How?

It is not what I have possessed or my position that has made this possible, but by helping others and by being helped. To help is to give and by giving I am helped in return. In one prayer, God asked me never to sell anything - only to give. Why?

The HELP Consciousness is God's Gift to

humanity and to sell you your gift would be in violation of my covenant with God.

Giving is the most powerful act of helping others and that activates The Law of Return and resources the fulfilment of your dreams. When you give, you are given a hundred fold. When you sell only the sale price returns to you.

If that is true, why do even the most spiritual leaders in your land *sell* their message and products? Because of the fear and doubt that if they give their sermons, seminars, training and books as gifts, they will not be returned - come back a hundred fold.

In *every* religion God has made it clear that what you give will come back to you a hundred fold. That makes giving the most prosperous way to become wealthy. So you see, it is not necessary to sell *anything* to resource the fulfilment of your dreams.

Anyone who sells anything to resource their God given dreams, will never have enough to make it come true. Why? Because selling, affirms that God will not *give* you the resources to realize your dream. That is why so many spiritual leaders and their organizations are driven to sell.

To fulfil your dreams, you need to increase your giving until you are free of selling. Pray and ask God to guide your giving and have faith that it will come back one hundred fold.

There was once a time in my life, when all I had was a handful of coins and the dream of diffusing The HELP Consciousness world-wide felt overwhelming.

As I prayed, God asked me to give the money away as a gift. This act of giving released a handful of coins into the world's money system which keeps coming back to finance The HELP Programme.

Giving according to God's will is like planting seeds in the most fertile soil. Gifts that are 'sown' in this way grow, bear fruit, multiply and come back to the giver as blessings. When this happens, your every desire will manifest miraculously.

This may seem impossible in a world where borrowing and selling are the main means of financing the fulfilment of your dreams. Not so, because that is exactly what is happening with my dream of creating Pan Paradise on Earth.

I do not borrow money or sell anything and yet I can afford to give countless books away. How? Everything I have is a gift from God, and by giving everything according to the will of God, I am given all I need, dream and desire.

Is your dream a gift from God?

If so, then with it comes all that is necessary to make your dream come true. By letting God guide your giving - helping, you will help yourself to realize all of your dreams.

The Third Level of Self-responsibility is to manifest your desires. When God gives you a dream, it gives rise to the desire to manifest it.

A real desire is of divine origin.

That is why real desires contain the 'word' of

God in their intention. A real desire by its very nature is totally pure in its intention to help - love.

If your desires are born of illusions they will never manifest fully. You see whenever God is not present in the creation of dreams and desires, the message and method of manifestation is a lie - false. That is why so many who avoid the guidance of God in their dreams fall by the wayside.

My desire is to help humanity live in peace and ease - Paradise. This appears impossible and it is if I try to do it myself. But with God's help, my desire is manifesting.......miraculously.

To manifest your desires, you have to begin with God, who will guide and give you all the resources you need to manifest your desires. By being with God, you are helping yourself in the manifestation of your desires. The ultimate act of helping yourself, is to devote your Self to God.

# *Message From The Author*

*Welcome to the house of HELP.*

As you read these words, you are participating in the biggest evolutionary leap our species has ever taken. By thinking of help, you are activating a very powerful force that is flowing around the Earth.

In this way, you are taking part in a world-wide programme for the creation of Paradise here and now. Is Paradise possible? Yes. Looking at our past, we can see that when people helped each other, the impossible became possible.

*Helping each other is the way*
*we will create Pan Paradise on Earth.*

As we enter the new millennium, over one thousand million people are living in poverty. How To HELP Your-*Self* was created by The HELP

Programme to help you meet all your needs and turn poverty into a living paradise.

The HELP Programme does not have a leader or following, an organization, hierarchy, or membership. The HELP Consciousness is not a religion, but a direct relationship with God - maintained by helping each other.

Helping each other releases the indwelling spirit of God that flows outward - amongst your family, friends, groups, organizations and nations around the Earth.

In this way, The HELP Consciousness flows like a wave from person to person via helpful actions. Now the wave has reached you. The more you learn how to help your Self, the more you will be able to help others.

An act of help is a gift. Helping has no gain or glory. You do it, just to do it. How can you help? If you have found How To HELP Your-*Self* useful, then you may want to give it to someone as a *gift*.

# HELP SEMINARS

Having read this book you, may be inspired to develop your practice of The HELP Process. For this purpose we conduct HELP Seminars as follows:

## *Schools, Colleges & Universities*

As parents and teachers, the first concern we have is to help our children. The HELP Seminars help students to help themselves. The HELP Process will become their helping hand for life.

## *Alternative health & welfare centres*

Are you involved in a helping profession? The HELP Seminars actually increase your capacity to help yourself and your clients. The HELP Process is currently being used by therapists, counsellors, healers and trainers.

## *Social & commercial organizations*

The HELP Seminars harness human potential and promote synergy in the work place, giving rise to increased creativity, productivity and prosperity. The HELP Process is being used by leaders, managers and administrators in many organizations internationally.

*For further information and bookings please write to:*

**HELP UK**
**P.O. Box 929 ~ Wimbledon ~ London ~ SW19 2AX ~ UK**

**HELP USA**
**P.O. Box 230056 ~ Boston ~ MA 02123-0056 ~ USA**

**HELP Australia**
**10 Kookaburra Park Eco - Village**
**MS 368 ~ Gin Gin ~ Qld ~ 4671 ~ Australia**

# TO RECEIVE YOUR FREE *GIFT* COPY
# OF HOW TO HELP YOUR-SELF

*Please send a large*
*Stamped Self Addressed Envelope*
to:
HELP (UK)
P.O. Box 929 ~ Wimbledon
London ~ SW19 2AX ~ UK


# TO HELP SUPPORT THIS WORK

Please send your:
Ideas and contributions to:
HELP Books International
P.O. Box 929 ~ Wimbledon
London ~ SW19 2AX ~ UK

*email: mail@helpbooksint.com*
*www.helpbooksint.com*

# HELP BOOKS INTERNATIONAL

To receive your free gift copy of this book or to become a distributor or co-ordinator in the country of your choice please write to:

**\*HELP UK**
P.O. Box 929
London
SW19 2AX
United Kingdom

**\*HELP Australia**
10 Kookaburra Park Eco - Village
MS 368 Gin Gin
Qld 4671
Australia

**\*HELP USA**
P.O. Box 230056
Boston, MA
02123-0056
USA

**HELP Australia**
1257 Riversdale Rd
Box Hill South
Victoria 3128
Australia

**HELP USA**
2565 West Grand Blvd
Suite 506
Detroit, Michigan 48208
USA

**HELP Australia**
5 Raleigh St
Atarman
Sydney 2064
Australia

**HELP USA**
2936 Corte Del Becero
Santa Fe
New Mexico 87505
USA

**\*HELP New Zealand**
7B Boyce St
Motueka
New Zealand

**HELP USA**
431 NE Alder St.
Yachats, Oregon 97498
USA

**\*HELP Canada**
NO:19 - 15875 - 84th Ave
Surrey BC
Canada 735 2N8

**HELP Canada**
26 Lambertlodge Avenue
Toronto
Ontario
M6G 3Y8
Canada

**HELP Germany**
Uland Str 54
Augsburg 86157
Germany

**HELP Switzerland**
P.O. Box 153
Chemin En Ballegues
1066 Epalinges
Vaud,
Switzerland

**HELP New Zealand**
29 Gaine St
New Plymouth
New Zealand

**HELP Venezuela**
Apartado 637
San Cristobal ~ Tachira
Venezuela 5001 - A

**HELP Spain**
Apdo. de Correos 98
07840 Sta. Eulalia del Rio
Ibiza
Spain

**HELP France**
Bas St Genis
38710 Mens
France

**HELP France**
Le Moulin D'onclaire
Coux - Ardeche
France

**HELP Greece**
Savvas Bros
Skopelos Magnisias
Skopelos
Greece

**HELP Romania**
AL Tudor Nicolae
Nr.129 BL. 1003 C~SC. A ETJ.
1 Apt. 7, IASI
Romania

**HELP The Slovak Republic**
Havlickova 39
04001
Kosice
The Slovak Republic

**HELP Russia**
Rysovo Eco - Village Project
Hlopina Str. 9/3, 19
St. Petersburg
Russia

**\*HELP India**
6 Dev Baug
Bhavnagar
India

**HELP Hong Kong**
41 Homantin Street
3/F Kowloon
Hong Kong

**\*HELP Sri Lanka**
358/1/2 Jaya Mahal Building
Horana Rd
Papiliyana junction
Boralesgamuwa
Sri Lanka

**HELP Singapore**
20 Cairn Hill Circle
# 01 - 44 Cairn Hill Court
Singapore 229 769

**HELP Kenya**
P.O. Box 50315
Nairobi
Kenya

**HELP Jamaica**
Point Village,
Norman Manley Blvd, Negril
Jamaica

*~ For more addresses see our website ~*
*www.helpbooksint.com*

# HELP MISSION

> *"Create Pan Paradise on Earth."*
> *"Change the evolutionary direction of humanity*
> *from hunter-hunted to helper helped."*

In 1992, Raja the pioneer of The HELP Consciousness had a vision:

*'To create The HELP Book and distribute*
*120 million copies in one hundred and twenty nations,*
*in the next forty years, without an organization.'*

The HELP Book was published on the 1st May 1999 ~ May Day,
which also means: 'Save Our Souls' or 'a call for help.'
Since publication The HELP Book has been endorsed by some
of the most respected figures in this field:

**\* Dr Deepak Chopra ~ Author & Visionary**
**\* Eileen Caddy ~ Co-Founder of The Findhorn Foundation**
**\* Jayne Goddard ~ President of The Complementary Medical Association - U**

The HELP Book contains a process that increases our capacity
to give and receive help. As such, The HELP Process promotes co-operation
in every field of endeavour. Helping each other is the way we will overcome
every challenge on the personal and planetary level and
create Pan Paradise on Earth.

*Our aim is to help humanity*
*by distributing The HELP Books as gifts.*
*The HELP Consciousness is God's gift to humanity.*
*That is why The HELP Books can only*
*be given as gifts.*